A Cen

by
Harry Furniss

with
Anecdotes of W. G. Grace

THE HAMBLEDON PRESS

Published by The Hambledon Press
35 Gloucester Avenue
London NW1 7AX

ISBN 0 907628 57 5

Furniss, Harry
    A century of Grace.
    1. Grace, W.G.   2. Cricket players –
    England – Biography
    I. Title
    796.35'8'0924   GV915.G7

Printed in Great Britain at the University Press, Oxford
by David Stanford, Printer to the University

Back Cover: Caricature of Grace by Arthur Bryan (1890).
This caricature and the originals of the Harry Furniss drawings
are in the G. Neville Weston Collection.

CONTENTS

Dr. W.G. Grace
Had hair all over his face.
Lord! How the people cheered
When a ball got caught in his beard!

E.C. Bentley

ANECDOTES OF W.G. GRACE

W.G. Grace's advice to aspiring cricketers: 'Never read print; it spoils one's eye for the ball'.

William Hemingway was often to be found in the dressing-room with his back to the window reading Greek. When Hemingway on one occasion complained to W.G. about his own temporary lack of success, the Old Man replied, 'How can you expect to make runs when you are always reading? I am never caught that way.'

It was a gusty morning when a fast ball eluded W.G.'s bat and snicked a bail which fell to the ground. 'Windy day today, umpire', remarked Grace replacing the bail. 'Make sure it doesn't blow your cap off on the way back to the pavilion', was the umpire's reply.

During a match between Gloucester and Essex, W.G. survived a caught and bowled appeal, regarded by both sides as 'out', by insisting that it was a bump ball. Some time after this incident W.G. was bowled by Kortright, the Essex fast bowler, who knocked both middle and leg stumps out of the ground. As the Old Man walked off Kortright exclaimed, 'What, are you going? There's still one standing'. W.G. said that he had never been so insulted in his life, but the extra runs he had scored in the meanwhile were enough to decide the match.

When drawing up a batting order W.G. invariably used the verb 'to come' and not 'to go'. Thus he always told players, 'You come in such and such a wicket down', never, 'You go in such and such a wicket down'. This was no doubt due to the fact that as both an opening batsman and long-term occupier of the crease W.G. nearly always saw new batsmen coming to him, rather than watching them go out from the pavilion.

During a London County match a club cricketer was playing for W.G. for the first time. When asked what number he would like to bat, the young man answered, 'Well, Doctor, I don't mind, but I've never made a "duck" in my life'. W.G. looked at him searchingly and said, 'What! never made a blob in your life! then last is your place: you haven't played long enough!'

In a match during which W.G.'s brother E.M. appealed frequently but to no avail, W.G., as yet another appeal was turned down, said confidentially to the umpire, 'Never mind my brother, he's always appealing. Now when I appeal it *is* out.'

Once Fred Roberts, Gloucestershire's fast left-handed bowler, failed to appeal after hitting the batsman squarely on the knee. W.G. came over from square-leg at the end of the over and demanded, 'Why didn't you appeal, Fred?' 'Oh', said Fred, 'I was waiting for *you*.'

W.G. had a joke he liked to play on newcomers to his side. Getting up from table, he would stoop as though to pick up something and call out, 'Hullo, any one lost half a sovereign?' After a general fidgeting and examination of pockets all round, the newcomer might reply, 'Yes, Doctor, I think I have.' Whereupon W.G. would fling a coin at him saying, 'Well, there's a ha'penny of it I have just found'.

Once when playing at Hastings against a side containing the Yorkshire player Schofield Haigh, W.G. was asked by Haigh for permission to catch a train before the end of play. Just before the time when Haigh wanted to leave, W.G. was batting and Haigh fielding at short-leg. W.G. skied an easy catch to him; as Haigh ran to catch the ball W.G. cried, 'If you catch it, I shall not let you leave the field.' The result was that Haigh missed the catch and caught his train.

When tossing for the first time with captains he had not played against before, W.G. would call 'The Lady', and walk off to pad up, claiming victory for Queen Victoria on one side or Britannia on the other.

An August Bank Holiday crowd was waiting to applaud a Grace hundred against Sussex at Bristol when W.G. was 93 not out. To their surprise W.G. declared on that score. The reason was that in his first class career he had scored every number from 0 to 100 except for 93; this declaration completed his record.

W.G. was an unwilling public speaker. On his tour with
R.A. FitzGerald to Canada and the U.S.A. in 1872 he
was however required to make a number of speeches. At
the first banquet in Canada he addressed the company
thus: 'Gentlemen, I beg to thank you for the honour
you have done me. I never saw better bowling than I
have seen today, and I hope to see as good wherever I
go'. He delivered the identical speech at other banquets
in Canada, only varying the subject of his praise to
'better batting', 'better wickets' and 'prettier ladies', and
in America to 'better oysters'.
In later years when threatened by the demand for a
speech, he would say, 'I think I must give them one of
my Canadian speeches'.

W G. loved bowling and felt it impossible that he was
not about to take a wicket with each ball. Once during
a match at the Oval, when W.G. had been bowling at the
Pavilion end for many overs to no avail, the captain of
the side he was playing in came up to him and asked
him whether it might not be a good idea to change the
bowling, and if he had any thoughts about who should
be put on. W.G. thought hard for a minute and then said
completely seriously, 'I tell you what. I'll go on at the
other end'. It had not occurred to him for a moment
that he should be taken off.

James Shaw, the Nottinghamshire fast-bowler exclaimed
after a long stint of bowling at W.G., during which the
latter had stroked the ball to all parts of the ground, 'I
puts 'em where I likes, but he puts them where he likes.'

A patient once knocked at the door of W.G.'s house in Bristol: 'Is Dr. Grace in?' The reply came back quickly, 'Of course he's in; he's been batting since lunch-time on Tuesday'.

When talking about a difficult maternity case W.G. said: 'Well, the baby's dead and I'm afraid that there's very little hope for the mother, but I do believe that I shall pull the father through'.

A distracted mother of twins suspected that they had measles. W.G.'s advice was: 'Put 'em in bed together and don't bother me unless they get up to 208 for two before lunch'.

When playing a Twenty-Two of Grimsby, W.G. was last out having scored 399 out of 681. A telegram had earlier been delivered to him at the wicket announcing the birth of his second son, upon which he had called for champagne all round. After his innings he claimed to have scored one more 'for the baby'. His score was accordingly altered to 400, as which it stands in the records to this day.

The Hon. Alfred Lyttleton, the Middlesex and England wicket-keeper, claimed that W.G.'s was the dirtiest neck of any he had kept behind. W.G. seems not to have been particular about washing. Once on a tour of Australia in 1873 he was greeted by the proprietor of a shanty hotel: 'Pleased to meet yer, W.G., but we can't do you Sydney style, no bloody bathrooms and suchlike'. To which W.G. replied, 'That don't matter. We Graces ain't no bloody water-spaniels'.

W.L. Murdoch was once watching a long innings by W.G. on a gloriously hot day, during which the latter perspired heavily. Turning to a friend, Murdoch remarked, 'Just my luck! Look at the Old Man dripping. I shall have to bat on a wet wicket again.'

W.G. loved watching cricket at all levels. One day he came across several small boys playing on Durdham Downs in Bristol. He offered to give them a few hints on batting, only to be met with, 'Garn! Wot do an old man like you know about cricket?'

At the height of his career W.G. was once confronted by a chance acquaintance who enquired, 'Excuse me, but are you by any chance related to *the* Grace? W.G. looked the man up and down before replying, 'The answer's a lemon, Sir'.

When a small boy at Lord's demanded W.G.'s autograph, the latter remembered his face and said, 'But I gave you my autograph at Brighton a month ago'. The boy replied, 'I know, but I swopped you for Dan Leno and a couple of bishops'.

Such was W.G.'s domination of the game that numerous proposals were suggested to restore the balance. Amongst these were that he should in future play either blindfold or with his right arm tied behind his back; that he should be declared 'out' whenever the umpire liked; that he should always have to bat eleventh; and that he should either use a smaller bat or be not allowed to play.

Cricket Match — admission three pence. If Dr. W.G. Grace plays, admission six pence.

At a benefit match the umpire called 'not out' when W.G. was unexpectedly bowled for nought, explaining to the astounded bowler, 'They have all paid to watch Dr. Grace bat, not to see you bowl.'

W.G.'s letter to *The Sportsman*, 27 August 1914:

Sir, — There are many cricketers who are already doing there duty, but there are many more who do not seem to realize that in all probability they will have to serve either at home or abroad before the war is brought to a conclusion. The fighting on the Continent is very severe, and will probably be prolonged. I think the time has arrived when the county cricket season should be closed, for it is not fitting at a time like this that able-bodied men should be playing day after day, and pleasure-seekers look on. There are so many who are young and able, and are still hanging back. I should like to see all first-class cricketers of suitable age set a good example, and come to the help of their country without delay in its hour of need. Yours, etc., W.G. Grace.

W.G. died on October 26 1915 from a heart attack shortly after a Zeppelin raid. The Germans indeed claimed him as a war casualty. He had been unnerved by the Zeppelins and when told, 'You faced the fastest bowling on appalling wickets without flinching, so why are you afraid of the Zeppelins?', replied, 'But I could see the bowling, and I can't see those damned things'.

REMARKABLE ACHIEVEMENTS OF
W.G. GRACE

W.G. Grace scored 126 centuries in first class matches and 95 in minor matches

He carried his bat through a completed innings seventeen times.

He three times scored two separate hundreds in a match.

He five times scored three separate hundreds in successive first class matches.

He scored a hundred and took ten or more wickets in a match fourteen times.

He scored a thousand runs and took a hundred wickets in a season eight times; on two of these occasions he scored over two thousand runs.

He was never dismissed twice for 0 in a first class match.

On May 23, 24 and 25, 1895, W.G. (then aged 47) was on the field during every ball of the match. He made 257 and 73 not out and also took two wickets.

Grace once scored a century and took five wickets on ice, playing a match on the frozen lake in Windsor Great Park.

Year	Runs	Wickets	Year	Runs	Wickets
1865	197	20	1888	1886	93
1866	581	31	1889	1396	44
1867	154	39	1890	1476	61
1868	625	49	1891/2*	771	58
1869	1320	73	1892	448	5
1870	1808	50	1892	1055	31
1871	2739	79	1893	1609	22
1872	1561	68	1894	1293	29
1873	2139	106	1895	2346	16
1874	1664	140	1896	2135	52
1875	1498	191	1897	1532	56
1876	2622	129	1898	1513	36
1877	1474	179	1899	515	20
1878	1151	152	1900	1277	32
1879	993	113	1901	1007	51
1880	951	84	1902	1187	46
1881	917	57	1903	593	10
1882	975	101	1904	637	21
1883	1352	94	1905	250	7
1884	1361	82	1906	241	13
1885	1688	117	1907	19	–
1886	1846	122	1908	40	–
1887	2062	97			

*Australia

Total Runs in First Class Cricket	54,904
Total Runs in Minor Matches	44,936
Grand Total	99,840
Total Wickets in First Class Cricket	2879
Total Wickets in Minor Matches	4446
Grand Total	7325

HARRY FURNISS AND W.G. GRACE

Harry Furniss (1854-1925) was a well-known caricaturist notable for his illustrations of Dickens, Lewis Carroll's *Sylvie and Bruno*, and contributions to *Punch*. He gives the following account of how he came to draw these cartoons of Grace, first published in *How's That?* (1896).

Just as I got into my seat 'W.G.' walked out of the pavilion, accompanied by Mr. Stoddart, to open the game. I may mention that at this time the excitement was tremendous as to whether 'W.G.' would make another *century*. As luck would have it, the Champion was in fine form — playing in faultless style. By the time the day had finished, I had seen the renowned cricketer to perfection — I had seen him make his *century*. He was caught before he had progressed very far in the second hundred. I returned to my studio with the massive form of 'W.G.' well imprinted upon my brain. Now it is much easier for the most moderate cricketer to catch a batsman than it is for an artist or even a photographer. But I gave myself a task as soon as I returned, which, at the request of the popular publisher of this little book, who is a great admirer of cricket, I reluctantly now make public. I put before me a hundred half-sheets of notepaper, and, without any preliminary sketching or alteration, I undertook to make a hundred sketches of W.G. Grace from memory, one on each piece of paper, and if I failed with one I was 'caught out'. But I carried out my pencil, and my innings was closed as the clock struck the hour of midnight, although more than once during my inky innings I had, in fairness to the great Cricketer, to call out 'How's that?' for I feel that I have let myself off in my innings too frequently, as a glance at these rapid sketches will easily show.

HERE HE IS

COMING OUT

COVERING WICKET

MAKING A BLOCK

MAKING READY

READY

READY FOR ANY BOWLING

NOW THEN !

PLAYS FORWARD

LEFT TOE UP

SCIENCE

A STOLEN RUN

A BACK VIEW

A HIT TO LEG

A RUN SAVED

WINDED

RECOVERING

CAUTIOUS

OUT ! LEG BEFORE,
OF COURSE

FIELDING: A STUDY IN BACKS

BOWLING: ARRANGING THE FIELD

THE CHAMPION BOWLS

BUT NOT THE CHAMPION BOWLER

FIELDING

OH !

AH !

HA ! HA !

POINT

SAVING A RUN

THE THREE STAGES OF A CATCH

IMPATIENT

NOT QUITE

STOPPED

WELL FIELDED

A WAY HE HAS

HOW'S THAT?

COMING IN AGAIN

THE BLOCK

THE TURF

PATTING THE CREASE

HIS FIRST OVER

NOT YET!

TAKING IT EASY

CAREFUL

CUTTING

A RUN

FOR FOUR

BLOWN

WARM WORK

WARM WORK

WARM WORK

IS IT A RUN?

GINGERLY

NOT FOR W. G. !

A CRACK

A BLOW

IN FULL BLAST

IN FULL BLAST

IN FULL BLAST

A NASTY ONE

BLOCK

TO THE BOUNDARY

WATCHING IT

THE USUAL TELEGRAM

AT REST

AT REST .

PILING IT UP

A BIT FAGGED

HOT

NOT HIS OVER

READY FOR A SWIPE

SAVED !

THAT CREASE AGAIN

WAITING FOR A
RICHARDSON

NO ! NO !

LATE

OUT!　100

TO THE PAVILION

THE FINAL BOW